THE
BATTLE
IS ON!

SPIRITUAL
MARTIAL ARTS

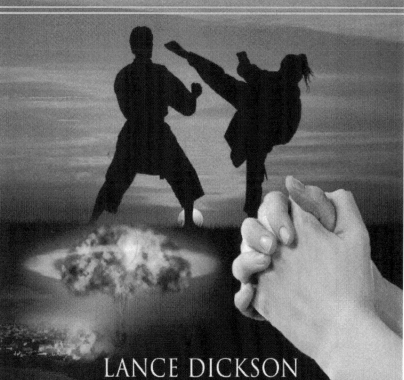

LANCE DICKSON

PREFACE

I am writing this book to provide readers with tools to use as you may engage in Spiritual Warfare. This is not a book for the faint hearted. This is not a book for those who have not embraced their faith in Jesus Christ. Spiritual Warfare is real, and the intensity of the attacks can be overwhelming. As I write this book I am currently under a spiritual attack.

Earlier, I almost gave in to the pressures of what was happening in my life. Let me give you some information so you can have an idea about what is going on. Three months ago, I published a book called "Grace Mercy & Faith – The Keys to Spiritual Empowerment: An Educational Perspective". I have been sharing the book with various people all of whom has given me great reviews. The reviews were so overwhelming that I was interviewed on a radio program and was later scheduled to have another discussion regarding additional content of the book. Additionally, it was on the best sellers list of spiritual books on Amazon. As I wrote this this book, I knew that the contents were not something that Satan wanted the masses to read.

I anticipated some spiritual attacks designed to prevent me from going forward and sharing this message. This anticipation was mental, something that was intellectualized in my mind. When these attacks began, I was not spiritually prepared to deal with them.

The attacks were on a variety of different fronts, relationships, finances, personal issues, and more. They all came at once and it was overwhelming. The problem was my inability about how to engage in spiritual warfare.

As I started to think about this writing, I began to remember the forward of my previous book: Grace Mercy & Faith. It shared information many of the trials I experienced. As a reader I am sure you wondered "Why things had not improved in his life?"

With the publishing of my last book I expected to write more information about victory instead, I am writing about satanic attacks. Fortunately, through God's grace, I was exposed to information that allowed me to see what was happening. Once the picture was clear and I knew what was going on, I became angry. This time my anger was directed in the right places.

As a Martial Artist, the words to my students, were just because I don't like to fight doesn't mean I don't know how to fight. In this case, I did not know how to fight, and was taken a beating. Thus, I began the writing of this book and now I am sharing how to engage in spiritual warfare. As I stated earlier, this is not going to be a book for the fainthearted, but for those in a spiritual battle and desiring the victory

There are many Christians who are fearful of engaging in spiritual warfare. They are fearful of the enemy's tactics which he will use against them. The one thing that I will say to those who may have those feelings of fear is "Satan will attack you whether you engage in spiritual warfare or not". As a follower of Jesus Christ remember, you are Satan's enemy.

You can choose to allow Satan to attack and attempt to destroy you or you can choose to learn how to fight back. Personally, I got so angry at what was happening and the reason why it was happening that I chose not only to learn how to fight back but to fight on the behalf of those who are unaware of how to fight. This is the reason behind this book!

There are certain events that take place in a person's life where you can anticipate some type of demonic attack. Those events are:

1. *Times of Spiritual Growth*
2. *Invading Enemy Territory*
3. *Exposing the Enemy*
4. *Breaking with the World*
5. *Blessings to Come*

Chip Ingram: The Invisible War

In my case, I had just finished the book Grace Mercy and Faith which put me in numerous categories regarding anticipating a satanic attack. I was growing spiritually as I was listening to God regarding what I was writing. I was exposing the enemy by sharing God's word in a known new and unique way.

I also was expecting blessings due to the anticipated exposure of this book. I should have known and been prepared for the demonic attacks which I faced. As a Martial Artist I have learned numerous things regarding managing conflict everything from avoidance to engaging in battle.

I first applied my martial arts experience and skills in the area of education. In my book Mental Martial Arts, I explained how certain martial arts concepts can be used with educational principals to combat some of the challenges we experience in life. In this book I will use some of those same concepts to aid as you study God's word and apply the wisdom contained in the bible to combat spiritual attacks.

Prior to getting into the content of this book let me share with you one little secret that should provide you with a little encouragement as you continue. This war that you have become a part of has already been won by Jesus Christ. You already have the victory! You need to learn is how to walk in that victory.

Once you complete this reading, not only will you be prepared to engage in spiritual warfare, but you will be able to share this information and help others fight this battle. As I stated in a previous book, mentally I anticipated an attack, but was not spiritually prepared to deal with it.

My recommendation is that before you engage in reading this book, accept Jesus Christ as your Lord and Savior. Get established with a local body of believers (church) so that you can be taught. Have a personal Bible available to read God's word and learn about our Father. Lastly, I recommend reading my book "Grace Mercy & Faith – The Keys to Spiritual Empowerment: An Educational Perspective" prior to engaging in this one. It will give you a solid foundation as you engage in this battle with the enemy. The book contains a lot of guidance about reading and studying the Bible, and what's available to you because of God's grace mercy and faith.

Contents

UNDERSTANDING
THE BASICS

THE DECISION TO ENGAGE IN BATTLE

The decision to engage in a battle is always preceded by some form of conflict. That conflict can be the initiation of an aggressive action or behavior. When a person is oppressed, and aggressive behavior is being forced upon them, a response to that behavior can be either fight or flight. When we make the decision to fight it will usually end with battle or war.

When deciding to engage in a battle, this decision should never be taken lightly. Battle and war always will result in some sort of loss. This loss could range from a loss of relationships to the loss of life. In the case of spiritual warfare, this battle was forced upon us. When we made the decision to accept Christ as our Lord and savior, we became targets of Satan's attacks.

"Be sober, be vigilant; Because your adversary the devil, as a roaring lion, walketh about, seeking whom he may devour."

1 Peter 5: 8

As a Christian you have become a part of an eternal battle between the forces of Satan and the forces of God. When you made the choice to accept God's gift of Salvation through the sacrifice of his son Jesus Christ, you became a target of the enemy.

You will be attacked. The decision you must make is how you will respond to these attacks. You can choose to endure the attacks which will lead to much strife and heartache, or you can choose to exercise your God given authority and learn how to fight back. The choice is yours, but for those who want to learn how to engage in this battle continue to read on.

Now that you have made the decision not to be victimized by Satan and his tactics, there is a certain amount of information that you need to be aware. First you must understand the enemy. Who are you fighting against? Whenever the military engage in any form of conflict, an understanding of the enemy's capabilities and tactics is essential information that is necessary to ensure a victorious outcome.

Thus, we may say that if you know yourself and know your enemy, you will gain victory a hundred times out of a hundred. If you know yourself but do not know your enemy, you will meet one defeat for every victory. If you know neither yourself nor your enemy, you will never be victorious.

Sun Tzu: The Art of War

Making the decision to engage in battle is always made with the goal of victory in mind. We don't choose to fight a battle expecting to lose. One essential fact that we must keep in mind when we engage in spiritual warfare is the victory of this war has already been obtained through Jesus Christ's sacrifice on the cross.

He will swallow up death in victory; and the Lord God will wipe away tears from off all faces; and the rebuke of his people shall he take away from off all the earth: for the Lord hath spoken it.

Isaiah 25:8

But thanks be to God, which giveth us the victory through our Lord Jesus Christ.

1 Corinthians 15:57

If the victory of this war has already been obtained through Jesus Christ sacrifice on the cross, then why is there a need for battle? In order to answer this question, let's review an event that took place in the months after World War II. Japan announced its surrender from World War II on August 15, 1945 and it was formally signed on September 2, 1945.

Although Japan formally signed a surrender, the battle continued until the Treaty of San Francisco was implemented on April 28, 1952. The Treaty of San Francisco was a peace treaty between Japan and the Allied Powers which was signed on September 8, 1951.

The surrender of Japan was signed in 1945 but the fighting continued for nearly seven more years because there were Japanese factions that continued to fight after the surrender. They either did not believe the surrender was valid or refused to accept the surrender based on the code that they followed.

This is an example of what we are dealing with as we engage in Spiritual Warfare with the satanic forces of the enemy. As with Japan, even though the war was officially over with Japan's surrender, the fighting continued which still resulted in loss of life or injury to personnel. When we are engaged in battle with the enemy you will still be attacked regardless of the fact that Satan was defeated at the cross.

The thief cometh not, but to steal, and to kill, and to destroy. I am come that they might have life, and that they might have it more abundantly.

John 10:10

The thief is one of the many names that the bible uses to describe Satan. The scripture clearly states that his intention is to steal, kill, and destroy. Although Jesus has defeated Satan on the cross, that does not prevent him from attacking the believer. These attacks are real and can result in much pain and heart ache.

Understanding who the enemy is and the tactics he will use is the preparation needed when these attacks are initiated against you. Another thing to consider when you have to engage in any type of conflict or battle is what are your own capabilities? The Word of God has numerous instances where it explains what you can do when exposed to Satanic attacks.

Knowing your God given authority is essential when engaging in spiritual warfare. Just like there are tactics that Satan and his demonic forces attempt to implore against you, there are tactics that God has made available to you as a believer to resist the advances of the enemy.

KNOW YOUR ENEMY

When dealing with the topic of Spiritual Warfare, we know that Satan is the name of our enemy. However, many are unaware of the capabilities of our enemy. They are also unaware that our enemy goes by many names in addition to the common name of Satan which we all are aware.

Many have a lack of knowledge of the history or background of the enemy. Finally, many are unaware of the battle tactics that the enemy will implore against them. We need to understand all these areas in order to effectively engage in Spiritual Warfare.

Otherwise we will be vulnerable to the attacks of the enemy and experience much loss and heartache. One of the first things we need to know about the enemy is his background. Who is he and how did he become our enemy?

Answering this question requires going to a specific passage of scripture which describes the origin of Satan. Many refer to Ezekiel 28:11-19 when speaking of the origin of Satan. The scripture describes a being that was full of wisdom and perfect in beauty. He was present in the garden of Eden and was the anointed cherub set by God.

Cherub - a winged angelic being described in biblical tradition as attending on God. It is represented in ancient Middle Eastern art as a lion or bull with eagles' wings and a human face and regarded in traditional Christian angelology as an angel of the second highest order of the nine-fold celestial hierarchy.

Oxford Dictionaries© Oxford University Press

He was upon the holy mountain of God and walked up and down in the midst of the stones of fire. He was perfect in his ways from the day he was created until iniquity was found in him. This passage of scripture also describes God's judgement and Satan's fall when it states how his heart was lifted up because of his beauty.

How he corrupted his wisdom because of his brightness. How he defiled his sanctuaries by the multitude of his iniquities. The scripture states how God will destroy the covering cherub from the midst of the stones of fire.

How he will be cast to the ground laid before kings to see. God will bring forth a fire from the midst which will devour and bring him to ashes upon the earth in the sight of all. The challenge with this passage of scripture is that there are certain biblical scholars who believe that this scripture is not referring to Satan.

The dispute is that in verse 12 the scripture specifically states "Son of Man, take up a lamentation upon the king of Tyrus, (a historical figure) and say unto him, Thus saith the Lord God;..."

Those who hold on to the belief that this passage of scripture is in fact the origin of Satan states that there is no way that an earthly man could have been a cherub set by God and present in the Garden of Eden as described in the scripture. The other viewpoint is that those descriptions were more poetic and not truly factual. Each group provides numerous viewpoints to support their stance on this scriptural passage.

The following is a viewpoint that I would like you to consider by exploring certain facts that we can establish through the Bible. First is that in addition to this physical world that we live in there is also an invisible world that exist. In the book "The Invisible War by Chip Ingram" he speaks of scriptures in both the Old and New Testament that refers to the existence of this invisible world.

In 2 Kings 6:15-19 the servant of Elisha was afraid due to the number of horses and chariots the King of Syria sent for Elisha. Elisha response was not to be afraid because there was more with him than what the King of Syria sent, then he prayed to God to open his servant eyes so that he may see.

Once God responded to Elisha prayer his servants was able to see horses and chariots of fire in the invisible world that was with Elisha. In Colossians 1:15-16 the scripture speaks of the invisible God who created everything in heaven and earth, visible and invisible, whether they be thrones, or dominions, or principalities, or powers: all things were created by him.

On numerous occasions through Jesus ministry he spoke to unclean spirits to either command them to release people who were possessed or to rebuke those who are being influenced by them.

On one occasion in Mark 8:33 and in Matthew 16:23 scripture described how Jesus said to his disciple Peter "Get thee behind me Satan" after Peter made a comment forbidding Jesus to give his life. Was Jesus calling Peter Satan or was he speaking directly to the Spirit that was influencing Peter to make that comment?

If we can accept as fact that an invisible world exist and that Jesus spoke directly to the Spirit of Satan when he said to Peter "Get thee behind me Satan", then can we accept as fact that the profit Ezekiel was speaking to the Spirit of Satan when God commanded him to take up a lamentation upon the king of Tyrus?

Apart from the origin and fall of Satan as described in Ezekiel 28:11-19, there are several other passages of scripture that can aid us in knowing about our enemy. Satan is referred to by many titles and names throughout the bible. The following is just a few of the many names and titles that has been attached to our enemy.

1. Thief

John 10:10 specifically states the desires of the enemy regarding our lives opposed to the desires of Jesus. Satan's desire is to kill and destroy us whereas Jesus desire is for us to have an abundant life.

The thief cometh not, but for to steal, and to kill, and to destroy. I am come that they might have life, and that they might have it more abundantly.

John10:10

2. Beelzebub

Mathew 12:24 describes the name Beelzebub as the Prince of Devils. In Mathew 12:25,26 Jesus confirms that Beelzebub is a name for Satan.

But when the Pharisees heard it, they said, this fellow doth not cast out devils, but by Beelzebub the Prince of the devils.

Mathew 12:24

3. Father of Lies

John 8:44 describes some of the characteristics of Satan. Specifically, being the father of lies.

Ye are of your father the devil, and the lusts of your father ye will do. He was a murderer from the beginning, and abode not in the truth, because there is no truth in him. When he speaketh a lie, he speaketh of his own: for he is a liar, and the father of it.

John 8:44

4. The God of this World

Scripture describe how the gospel of Christ is hidden to those who are lost or do not believe in the message of Christ because Satan has blinded their minds.

In whom the god of this world hath blinded the minds of them which believe not, lest the light of the glorious gospel of Christ, who is the image of God, should shine unto them.

2 Corinthians 4:4

Satan also confirms his status of the god of this world when he attempted to tempt Jesus in the wilderness by offering him all the kingdoms of the world to worship him.

And the devil taking him up into an high mountain, and shewed unto him all the kingdoms of the world in a moment of time. And the devil said unto him, All this power will I give thee, and the glory of them: <u>for that is delivered unto me</u>; and to whomsoever I will I give it. If thou therefore wilt worship me, all shall be thine.

Luke 4:5-7

5. Adversary

1 Peter 5:8 gives a warning to all believers as it describes what Satan is seeking to do to us.

Be sober, Be vigilant; because your adversary the devil, as a roaring lion, walketh about, seeking whom he may devour

1 Peter 5:8

There are numerous other names and titles throughout the Bible that describe aspects of our enemy. Generally, each name can give some insight to a characteristic of the enemy. As we review the Bible and explore the many different ways that is used to describe Satan, we can gain a better understanding and knowledge of the enemy's characteristics as we prepare for battle.

Thus, we may say that if you know yourself and know your enemy, you will gain victory a hundred times out of a hundred. If you know yourself but do not know your enemy, you will meet one defeat for every victory. If you know neither yourself nor your enemy, you will never be victorious.

Sun Tzu: The Art of War

In order to really be successful in this battle we need to truly understand who we are facing and the extent of his capabilities. Additionally, we need to understand the extent of our capabilities and know how we can engage in this battle.

THE ENEMY'S BATTLE TACTICS

There are numerous tactics that Satan utilizes against the believer. His goal is to kill, steal, and destroy our lives. We must understand his tactics so we can be prepared to fight against them. In many cases these tactics are so subtle that you may not even realize that an attack has been initiated against you. As we continue, a number of the tactics that Satan and his demonic force uses will be identified. Satan's purpose for these tactics will also be shared.

Tactic Number 1 – Deception

Deception is probably the primary tactic of the enemy and he is a Master at it. Satan's lies dates back to the Garden of Eden when he deceived Eve into disobeying a commandment from God by eating from the tree of the knowledge of Good and Evil. Satan is a liar and has been described as the Father of lies. What makes his lies effective is that in many cases they are mixed with a strand of truth.

In some cases, the lies of the enemy are spread about by sources that you may consider reliable. These people may be totally unaware that the information that they are sharing is false. One of the main reasons for the lies of Satan is to prevent people from knowing the truth of God's word.

But if our gospel be hid, it is hid to them that are lost. In whom the god of this world hath blinded the minds of them which believe not, lest the light of glorious gospel of Christ, who is the image of God, should shine unto them. 2 Corinthians 4:4

The lies of Satan keep people from knowing the truth of God's word thus keeping them in a bondage that they are not even aware exist. These lies are transferred to people from other people who are unaware of the falsehood that they are spreading or via thoughts that Satan shares with men by injecting thoughts into their minds via the spiritual world.

The power of God and our God given authority lies within God's word. Everything that we need to resist and defeat the attacks of the enemy is contained in the word of God. The truth of God's word is the thing that Satan fears.

And ye shall know the truth, and the truth shall make you free.

John 8:32

Tactic Number 2 – Doubt

Doubt - a feeling of uncertainty or lack of conviction.

Doubt is the tactic that Satan will use against you when he is unable to deceive you regarding the promises of God. One of Satan's greatest weapon is doubt. Doubt in God and His word. Doubt in God's promises and doubt in your own abilities.

If Satan can introduce doubt into your mind, he can hinder your ability to apply truth of God's word to your life. Doubt is always based on some type of lie or deception that Satan implants in our mind. Doubt will short circuit and hinder your application of faith.

Tactic Number 3 – Circumstances of Life

Because we live in a natural world, we have a mandate to comply with the rules and regulation of that natural world. Circumstances which in many cases are legitimate tends to take our time away from the things we need to do to live according to God's word. It takes our time from studying and reading God's word; it takes our time from praying to the Holy Spirit for guidance.

The power of these circumstances is that they are legitimate. Because we live in a natural world, we tend to focus on those things that we can experience through our five natural senses. Those things that we can't explain, those things that are not bound by our five senses we tend to put in the background, thus limiting our power to achieve the abundant life that God promises.

These circumstance alone are not necessarily due to demonic influences. There are some circumstances that are orchestrated by demonic influences and others that are just a result of the natural world in which we live.

In either case the enemy will attempt to interject thoughts into your mind designed to lead you in a direction contrary to the will of God. If you accept these thoughts as truth you will be headed down a path that not only can be contrary to God's will but in some cases could have a devastating effect on your life.

Tactic Number 4 – Passivity

This is the tactic that Satan exploits to gain ground and control of your mind and behavior. This is a most dangerous tactic because in many cases the individual never sees it as an attack from the enemy.

Passivity is a result of us not exercising our mind or our will and accepting without questioning any thought that is interjected into our thinking process. God created us as a spirit, containing a soul and a body.

Specifically, we are a spirit we have a soul and we live in a physical body. The original intention of God was for our spirit to have dominion over our soul and for our soul to direct the functions of our body.

One of the greatest gifts that God gave to man was free will. This is a function of the soul which is contained in our minds. Mankind has the ability to choose. Through the soul we can choose to obey and submit to the word of God or to reject his guidance. No thoughts can be forced upon us against our will whether that thought is from God or demonic forces.

Man is not an automaton that turns according to God's will. Rather, man has full sovereign power to decide for himself. He possesses the organ of his own volition and can choose either to follow God's will or to resist him and follow Satan's will instead.

Watchman Nee: The Spiritual Man

We should be able to choose and control any thoughts that is injected into our thinking process. Passivity is when we choose not to exercise our will. Thus, our will becomes weak and we accept thoughts that are contrary to what we want in our lives.

A sign that demonic forces has gained ground in the battlefield of our mind is when we can't control our thoughts. If we are unable to reject a thought that is contrary to the will of God, then demonic forces have gained a foothold in the battlefield of the mind.

Man's will and spirit are like a citadel which the evil spirits craved to capture. The open field where the battle is wage for the seizure of the Citadel is man's mind. Watchman Nee: The Spiritual Man

Tactic Number 5 – Sin

Sin – Transgression of the law of God

The tactic of sin is the one tactic of the enemy that everyone is familiar. Yet it is probably the most effective tactic of Satan. In most cases, the commission of sin is something that we choose to do. In many cases, we are well aware of the fact that we are committing a sin, but we choose to do it anyway. If we believe and trust in God, then why do we make a choice to commit a transgression against his law?

One of the reasons that man chooses to sin is that we are enticed by the enemy. As Satan enticed Eve in the Garden of Eden by interweaving a lie with a strand of truth. Satan promised Eve wisdom by having the knowledge of good and evil (Strand of Truth) even though this wisdom was forbidden by God. Satan also stated that she would not surely die (Lie, she died spiritually) and by having this knowledge that she will be like God (Lie).

Another reason that man chooses to sin is that in some cases the act of sin appeals to the flesh or body. An example would be sexual immorality. The sin of going beyond the God-given right of participating in the act of sex. Satan's tactic with sin is to entice us to commit the sin and once that has been accomplished, to condemn us for the commission of sin. His purpose is to discourage us, deceive us, and to sway us from following God's will for our lives.

Tactic Number 6 – Intellect & Reasoning

Understanding how the intellect and reasoning abilities of man can be used as a tactic of the enemy requires a knowledge of how our intellect and reasoning abilities operate within our minds.

The mind of man is his organ of thought. Through it he is equipped to know, think, imagine, remember, and understand. Man's intellect, reasoning, wisdom and cleverness all pertain to the mind. Broadly speaking the mind is the brain.

Watchmen Nee: The Spiritual Man

As stated previously, God created us as a spirit, containing a soul, and living in a physical body. The spirit, soul, and body all have different functions which aids us as we relate to the world. The spirit is how we relate to God in the spiritual world.

God is a Spirit: and they that worship him must worship him in spirit and in truth.

John 4:24

The body is how we relate to the natural world and the soul is the medium between the spirit and the body. Man's ability to reason and use his intellect is part of the function of the soul. The functions of the soul are volition, intellect, and emotion. The soul is how we interpret and understand the sensations of the body as well as the revelations of the spirit.

As stated previously, God's original intention was for our spirit to have dominion over our soul and for our soul to direct the functions of our body. The fall of man resulted in the death of our spirit. Our soul therefore took dominion with no guidance or direction from God.

Through our intellect and reasoning abilities we followed our own direction rather than the direction of God. Jesus Christ's sacrifice on the cross resulted in the rebirth of the spirit. Our spirit was born again and additionally we were given the Holy Spirit to reside in us, guide us, and teach us the will of God.

How Satan uses our intellect and reasoning abilities as a tactic against us is by means of deception. Our souls have been sitting on the throne of our lives until the rebirth of our spirit.

All decisions that we made was based on our ability to relate to the natural world that we live in and to understand how the natural world processes work. In many cases this understanding is a result of our five senses.

Because we live in a natural world, we tend to focus on those things that we can experience through our natural five senses and those things that we can't explain, those things that are not bound by our five senses we tend to put in the background thus limiting our power to achieve the abundant life that God promises.

Lance Dickson: Grace, Mercy, & Faith: The Keys to Spiritual Empowerment

The knowledge and revelations that come from God are not based on what can be determined via our five senses. Satan wants us to accept the lie that if it can't be explained or verified via our five senses then it is not real and therefore should be disregarded. Generally, intellect and reasoning abilities are based on what we can understand within the natural world that we live. Satan doesn't want us to give dominion of our lives to our reborn spirit. He wants our soul to remain on the throne of our lives so that we will continue to make decisions based on his deceptions rather than the guidance of the Holy Spirit.

Tactic Number 7 – Desires

Another tactic that Satan uses against the believer are the desires of the believer. Are our desires bad? How can Satan use our desires against us when the Bible states that God will give us the desires of our hearts?

Delight thyself also in the Lord: and he shall give the desires of thine heart.

Psalms 37:4

Therefore, I say unto you, what things soever ye desire, when ye pray, believe that ye receive them, and ye shall have them.

Mark 11:24

This is true, God will give us the desires of our heart, but how Satan uses desires against us is when your desires are outside of the will of God. If Satan can inject a thought into your mind that entices a desire that is outside of the will of God, it can lead you down a path that can be very destructive in your life.

Our desires are a strong factor in motivating our behaviors.

Lance Dickson: Mental Martial Arts: Using Educational Principles to Combat Life Challenges

An example that we have used previously can also show how a wrong desire can be utilize by Satan to lead a person down a path of destruction. Satan enticed Eve in the Garden of Eden by promising Eve wisdom by having the knowledge of good and evil even though this wisdom was forbidden by God. The thought of having wisdom created a desire within Eve which motivated her behavior to eat fruit from the forbidden tree thus introducing sin into the world.

Tactic Number 8 – Fear

Fear – a distressing emotion aroused by impending danger, evil, pain, etc., whether the threat is real or imagined; the feeling or condition of being afraid.

Dictionary.com

There is an acronym that many have heard regarding fear. False Evidence Appearing Real. In many cases (but not all cases) this acronym can be true. Fear is a tactic that the enemy uses to limit the believer as he pursues the will of God. Fear has been described as the opposite of faith. Both fear and faith focus on something that has not been manifested in this physical world.

The distinction between the two is fear focuses on the negative aspect of something occurring whereas faith is focused on the positive aspect of what may occur. Fear is a dangerous and devastating tactic that the enemy uses against the believer. It cannot only limit what the believer strives to achieve in his life, but it can also be debilitating in a person's physical and mental health.

Fear weakens our immune system and can cause cardiovascular damage. It can lead to accelerated aging and even premature death. It can impair formation of long-term memories and cause damage to certain parts of the brain. Fear can interrupt processes in our brain that allow us to regulate emotions, read nonverbal cues and other information presented to us. Other consequences of long-term fear include fatigue, clinical depression, and PTSD.

University of Minnesota: Impact of Chronic Fear

Tactic Number 9 – Money

There are many who say and believe that money is the root of all evil. This is absolutely false. Money is neither good nor evil. It is the attitude regarding money which creates the problem. This statement that money is the root of all evil, many believe comes from Scripture. In actuality, what the scripture really state is:

For the love of money is the root of all evil: which while some coveted after, they have erred from the faith, and pierced themselves through with many sorrows.

1 Timothy 6:10

The way Satan uses money as a tactic against the believer is by orchestrating circumstances that will either increase the amount that a person has or decrease the amount. In the natural world many make decisions based on the level of money they can obtain.

Rather than trusting God to provide for the needs, they trust their level of money. When the level of money is lacking, people may make decisions to do wrong in order to get a level that is sufficient for the needs. When the opportunity exists to obtain a large amount of money, decisions could be made to obtain that large amount rather than pursuing a path of righteousness which limits the amount of money one can obtain.

Satan's goal with this tactic is to get the believer to make decisions based on money rather than God. He wants you to put your trust in money and not trust God to meet your needs. A person's attitude towards money is a very strong tactic of the enemy.

For the love of money is the root of all evil: which while some coveted after, they have erred from the faith, and pierced themselves through with many sorrows.

1 Timothy 6:10

Tactic Number 10 – Pride

Pride – A high or inordinate opinion of one's own dignity, importance, merit, or superiority, whether as cherished in the mind or as displayed in bearing, conduct, etc.

Pleasure or satisfaction taken in something done by or belonging to oneself or believed to reflect credit upon oneself.

Dictionary.com

Pride is the sin that resulted in Lucifer's fall from grace. This resulted in his being cast out of the kingdom of God and becoming Satan the enemy of mankind. Pride is when we focus on ourselves and our accomplishments, rather than focusing on the goodness of God. Pride and the negative effects of pride are consistently spoken of throughout Scripture.

Pride goeth before destruction, and an haughty spirit before a fall.

Proverbs 16:18

A man's pride shall bring him low: but honor shall uphold the humble in spirit.

Proverbs 29:23

For all that is in the world, the lust of the flesh, and the lusts of the eyes, and the pride of life, is not of the Father, but is of the world.

1 John 2:16

These are only a few of approximately 45 scriptures which deals with pride. How is it possible for the enemy to effectively use the tactic of pride against the believer when there is so much in Scripture that warns us about it? The simple answer to this question is that it is natural to feel good about ourselves and our accomplishments.

Where the enemy effectively uses the tactic of pride against us is by injecting thoughts which causes us to focus specifically on ourselves. Thus, we are not thinking about the grace or mercy of God which enable us to perform whatever task that we are proud about. Pride leaves God out of the equation.

Tactic Number 11 – Relationships

There are numerous relationships that we establish as we go through this journey called life. We have relationships with family, friends, coworkers and professional associates. The closer the relationship is to you; the more influence exist between the people within the relationship.

The enemy uses this tactic when the people we have relation-ships with influences us to follow a path that is outside of the will of God. The effectiveness of this tactic is that usually those who exert influence over you are supposed to have your best interest in mind.

The people who we care about and love can give us guidance that we will usually follow. We will listen to them because of the level of our relationship. In many cases the person who is giving you advice truly believe that he or she is looking out for your best interest.

An example that demonstrates this in scripture is when Sarai offered her handmaid to Abram so that he may have a child because she did not believe that she could give him a child.

Now Sarai Abrams wife bare him no children: and she had an handmaid, an Egyptian, whose named was Hagar. And Sarai said unto Abram, behold now, the Lord hath restrained me from bearing: I pray thee, go in unto my maid; it may be that I may obtain children by her. And Abram hearkened to the voice of Sarai.

Genesis 16:3,4

Sarai was making a major sacrifice by offering her handmaid to her husband. She definitely had Abrams best interest in mind because she knew that God promised Abram descendants. Abram made the choice to listen to his wife because of the closeness of their relationship.

The question he should have ask is if the advice of Sarai was in line with the will of God? Often because of the level of the relationship and the trust we have for the person, we will accept the advice rather than seeking God to see if the advice is aligned with his will.

Another example of the enemy's use of this tactic is when he influences someone such as a coworker to make decisions or exhibit behavior that is directed towards hindering or hurting you. In this case, the relationship you have with the person is not one of closeness or trust. The relationship could be one of a coworker or business associate.

The enemy could entice their behavior through jealousy, anger, and numerous other negative emotions. The overall goal of the enemy is to entice the person to exhibit behavior designed to hinder, hurt, or harm you.

"Be sober, be vigilant; Because your adversary the devil, as a roaring lion, walketh about, seeking whom he may devour."

1 Peter 5: 8

Tactic 12 – Confessions

The things we say can have a great impact on the path which our life may take. There are many in this world that does not realize the power of a confession. We are faced with a lot of negativity in our society.

We see and hear many negative things in this natural world. Scripture states that Faith comes by hearing and hearing the word of God, but the opposite is also true. A lack of faith and fear can be introduced into your Spirit as you continuously hear negative confessions.

Death and life are in the power of the tongue: and they that love it shall eat the fruit thereof.

Proverbs 18:21

The goal of the enemy is not only for you to hear these confessions, but to give the enemy more ground by speaking these things that you hear. Many times, we will make a confession due to a lack of knowledge that confirms what the enemy wants in our life. We make statements such as "This headache is killing me" without realizing the power behind the confession. There is spiritual power in the things that we say. We must be very careful not to confess negative things which we don't want in our lives.

Don't agree with the enemy. If you speak the words of the enemy, you are writing the words of the enemy on the table of your heart. The reason some people are so filled with fear is that they believe everything they see and hear on television.

Charles Capps: Faith and Confessions

Tactic 13 – Feelings

Our feelings are one of the three basic functions of the mind. Feelings can be either an emotional state based on input received from any of the five senses: seeing, hearing, touching, smelling, tasting or it can be a belief based on some prior thoughts.

Lance Dickson: Mental Martial Arts: Using Educational Principles to Combat Life Challenges

Generally, our feelings are motivated by external sources that we receive from our five basic senses. We can have positive and good feelings such as joy; happiness; and love or we can have negative and bad feelings such as anger; resentment; and hate. Because our feelings tend to be externally motivated, the enemy will orchestrate circumstances that will result in negative feelings. If we allow or accept these negative feelings, then he can intensify those feelings with demonic thoughts designed to cause you emotional pain. The overall goal of the enemy is to convince you to act on these negative feelings.

Tactic 14 – Unanswered Prayer

The tactic of unanswered prayer is what Satan uses to plant seeds of doubt and unbelief regarding God and his word. Satan wants to convince you to have an indictment regarding God's goodness. Thoughts such as:

1. God's word is not true
2. Does God really love me
3. I prayed and it did not work.

The enemy will try to get you to accept in order to hinder God's work in your life. What you view as an unanswered prayer may be a matter of timing because the answer to your prayer did not come on your timetable. It can also be a matter of trust because you're not certain that God is working on your behalf.

Tactic 15 – Dreams

We all have dreams throughout the course of our lives. On occasion these dreams can be vivid and intense where we visualize some form of conflict or danger. You wake up with a sense of dread and terror, your heart rate is elevated, your blood pressure rises. This is when the dream becomes a nightmare.

There are numerous scientific theories on the causes of dreams and nightmares. What we want to discuss is when our dreams are orchestrated by Satanic influences. When you are awake you can resist the thoughts that come from the demonic domain by using your will.

When we sleep, this is a time for your mind to rest and your body to be replenished. If demonic forces are allowed to attack you while you are sleeping, you can experience horrifying nightmares. Unless you are aligned with the spirit you can be vulnerable.

In order to protect yourself in this vulnerable state you have to pray. Ask God for protection while you are sleeping and at rest. We will go into more detail regarding your defenses as we continue but for now consider and meditate on the following verse if you are experiencing this type of demonic attack.

The angel of the Lord encampeth round about them that fear him, and delivereth them.

Psalm 34:7

There shall no evil befall thee, neither shall any plague come nigh thy dwelling. For he shall give his angels charge over thee, to keep thee in all thy ways. They shall bear thee up in their hands, lest thou dash thy foot against a stone.

Psalm 91 10-12

BUILDING UP YOUR DEFENSES

Spiritual Espionage

Espionage – the practice of spying or of using spies, typically by governments to obtain political and military information.

When using the term spiritual espionage, we are referring to the aspect of our lives that provides information to the enemy concerning who we are and our individual desires. This aspect can be considered being in partnership with the agenda of the enemy. These are subtle attacks that we don't even realize with a purpose to cause us to rebel against the will of God.

Previously, the tactics that the enemy uses against us were described. Some of these tactics are used in the area of spiritual espionage. In many cases, we may not recognize the work of the enemy and how he is implementing his attacks.

"My people are destroyed for lack of knowledge"

Hosea 4:6

A knowledge of the tactics that Satan use in the area of spiritual espionage is essential in recognizing when these attacks may occur. This knowledge will allow us to develop a defense network to use against them. When digging deeper into this area I found that the common core of Spiritual espionage is deception. We are deceived into thinking that our behavior is ok, fine, moral, and in some cases godly. There are five tactics that Satan use in the area of spiritual espionage.

1. Desires
2. Passivity
3. Pride
4. Relationships
5. Intellect/Reasoning

Satan's overall goal is to deceive us into behaving outside of the will of God. In the case of spiritual espionage, the goal of his tactics is to camouflage the operations of the enemy. What makes these tactics so effective is that in many cases we are unable to see anything that is wrong. The reason for this is we live in a natural world and focus on what is natural.

Spiritual concerns tend to take a backseat. Our intuition becomes dull as we focus on the things that can be detected with our five senses. Therefore, these subtle attacks go unnoticed. Let's explore how some of these areas of spiritual espionage can be utilize against followers of the teachings of Jesus Christ.

Desires

There are numerous verses in the bible which speaks about man's desires. Generally, they speak about how God will grant us our desires.

Delight thyself also in the Lord; and he shall give the desires of thine heart

Psalms 37:4

The fear of the wicked, it shall come upon him: but the desire of the righteous shall be granted.

Proverbs 10:24

Unfortunately, the desires of man can be corrupted. Especially when they are a result of wrong motivations.

What are wrong motivations for desire?

Selfishness, jealousy, anger, pride, and numerous other emotions can lead us astray when attached to our desires. An example would be that you desire a promotion at work. This desire is not based on the fact that you worked hard to earn it, but it is based on the fact that a coworker with less time on the job than you received a promotion.

The desire for a promotion is legitimate but the emotion behind the desire is not in line with God's will for you.

Passivity

Passivity is not a term that is common among those of us who speak the English language. The general definition for passivity is acceptance of what happens, without active response or resistance. The way this is used in the area of spiritual espionage is by deceiving a person to accept a thought as if it was coming from God, without examining it through the use of our God given abilities.

It is to be sorely lamented that so many Christians, unaware of the basic difference between the activities of evil spirits and that of the Holy Spirit, have unconsciously permitted the enemy to enter and occupy their minds.

Watchman Nee: The Spiritual Man

One of the greatest gifts that God gave man is our volition, otherwise known as our free will. The ability to choose. God does not want us to be robots or puppets. He created us with the ability to make decisions and willingly choose to have a relationship with him. God will not force his will upon us, nor can any other spiritual being force their will upon us. Evil spirits and demons cannot force anything upon us if we exercise our will.

Passivity occurs when we do not exercise our will and accept whatever is presented to us without question. This acceptance could be due to a lack of knowledge or deception. As Christians, we do not want to question what we believe to be the Holy Spirit. Yet God's word specifically states:

Beloved, believe not every spirit, but try the spirits whether they are of God: because many false prophets are gone out into the world.

1 John 4:1

God wants us to listen and be guided by the Holy Spirit, but this does not mean blindly accepting any thought that comes to mind without validating it through the word of God.

Pride

Pride is considered one of the seven deadly sins. Earlier it was stated the reason why the enemy can effectively use the tactic of pride against us is because it is natural to feel good about ourselves and our accomplishments. The problem with pride is that it can lead to a variety of other very destructive emotions and behaviors. Things such as self-centeredness; vanity; jealousy; arrogance; and an overinflated ego can all be the results of pride.

As stated earlier, pride removes God from the equation. Pride will place you on the throne of your own life. Pride prevents any form of humility. Some examples of behaviors that are associated with pride are:

1. *Difficulty admitting you are wrong*
2. *Hating Correction*
3. *Not asking for help, rejecting support*
4. *Taking on more than you can handle*
5. *Unforgiveness*
6. *Selfishness*
7. *Magnifying the sins of others*
8. *Lying*
9. *Rejecting the truth*

Neal Chester: Pride is the Problem

Relationships

People develop many relationships throughout the course of their lives. Professional, business, personal, family, and intimate are just a few of the different type of relationships that people can develop. The closer the relationships are to you the more the influence those relationships will have over you. One of the many ways that Satan and his demonic forces wages war against you is through subtle attacks via your relationships.

These attacks can be in the form of advice given to you from a close personal or intimate relationship. This advice will appear to be completely innocent, and in most cases, it is innocent and given with the best intentions of the person who provides it. The problem is that the person giving the advice is being influence by the enemy and the relationship that you have with the person is influencing you to accept the advice. These subtle attacks are designed to convince you to do the bidding of the enemy.

Intellect/Reasoning

Beware lest any man spoil you through philosophy and vain deceit, after the tradition of men, after the rudiments of the world, and not after Christ.

Colossians 2:8

Intellect and reasoning are functions of the mind which are used to make sense of the external stimulus that we receive from our five senses. As stated previously, the functions of the soul are volition, intellect, and emotion. The soul is what is used to interpret and understand the sensations of the body as well as the revelations of the spirit. Our intellect and reasoning abilities is how we do it.

Due to the fact that we use our intellect to interpret the stimulus from the natural world in which we live, we can choose not to refer to God or the Holy Spirit regarding anything that we attempt to interpret. The desire of the enemy is for us to use our intellect and reasoning abilities to guide us in how we live without including God or his word in the process.

When we choose not to include God or his word as we attempt to make sense regarding the world we live in, Satan can inject subtle thoughts into our thinking process designed to lead us in a direction outside of the will of God. We must make a conscious effort to remember to include God into our reasoning process. In this way we won't be led astray by the demonic forces of the enemy.

Spiritual espionage will always be subtle. Our biggest defense against these attacks is our knowledge. Being able to recognize the potential for an attack and actively deciding not to be deceived by the enemy.

THE WEAPONS OF OUR WARFARE

What is it that we need to understand about the weapons of our warfare?

First, we must understand the power behind our weapons. We need to understand the type of weapons available to us. Finally, we must know the purpose of our weapons in order to effectively use them against the enemy.

For the weapons of our warfare are not carnal, but mighty through God to the pulling down of strongholds; Casting down imaginations, and every high thing that exalteth itself against the knowledge of God, and bringing into captivity every thought to the obedience of Christ;

2 Corinthians 10:4,5

As we examine this scripture, we can see that the power behind our weapons is God. The type of weapons available to us is mighty and spiritual and the weapons that we use in our battle with the enemy has several purposes. Our weapons will break the strongholds of the enemy; cast down imaginations and everything that attempts to elevate itself above the knowledge of God; and forces every thought to be in obedience to Christ.

Another aspect of the weapons of our warfare is our battle armor. When we as followers of the teachings of Jesus Christ speak about our spiritual armor, we are speaking of Paul's description in Ephesians 6:10 – 17.

Finally, my brethren, be strong in the Lord, and in the power of his might. Put on the whole armor of God, that ye may be able to stand against the wiles of the devil. For we wrestle not against flesh and blood, but against principalities, against powers, against the rulers of the darkness of this world, against spiritual wickedness in high places. Wherefore take unto you the whole armor of God, that ye may be able to withstand in the evil day, and having done all, to stand. Stand therefore, having your loins girt about with truth, and having on the breastplate of righteousness; and your feet shod with the preparation of the gospel of peace; above all, taking the shield of faith, wherewith ye shall be able to quench all the fiery darts of the wicked. And take the helmet of salvation, and the sword of the spirit, which is the word of God.

Ephesians 6:10 – 17

The spiritual armor described in Ephesians consist of Six pieces:

1. The Belt of Truth
2. The Breastplate of Righteousness
3. The Sandals of the Gospel of Peace
4. The Shield of Faith
5. The Helmet of Salvation
6. The Sword of the Spirit.

The Belt of Truth

Stand therefore, having your loins girt about with truth,

One of the primary weapons that Satan uses against us is lies and deception. Our defense against this tactic is truth. We have to know the truth of God's word as we confront the lies of the enemy. We have to remember that the battlefield where we engaged the enemy is within our minds. The belt of truth is what protects us from demonic thoughts which the enemy attempts to get us to accept. The responsibility of putting on the belt of truth is ours and ours alone.

We are to train our minds to see God, ourselves, and others through the clear lens of what he says is true. That means that we don't play games. We're honest with God, honest with ourselves, and honest with others. We're open when the Spirit of God speaks to us. We don't allow ourselves to be deceived, and don't rationalize our sins away under the disguise of ignorance, relativity, or blame.

Chip Ingram: The Invisible War

The Breastplate of Righteousness

and having on the breastplate of righteousness

Putting on the breastplate of righteousness is about acknowledging your identity as a born-again believer. Our righteousness is from God and not of ourselves. We are righteous because God said we are righteous. It is not based on anything that we have done to deserve it. Our righteousness is based on the sacrifice of Jesus Christ.

For he hath made him to be sin for us, who knew no sin; that we might be made the righteousness of God in him.

2 Corinthians 5:21

The breastplate of righteousness protects us from the condemnation of the enemy. As a born-again believer we are no longer sinners, but we are the righteousness of God. There are many who describe themselves by saying that "I am a sinner saved by grace". This is no longer true. You were a sinner but now you are the righteousness of God. When we put on the breastplate of righteousness, we are shielding ourselves with the righteousness of God which is in Christ Jesus.

The breastplate of righteousness has a twofold application: Jesus is our Righteousness, and we put him on first. It also shows our obedience to the Word of God.

Kenneth E. Hagin: The Believers Authority

The Sandals of the Gospel of Peace

and your feet shod with the preparation of the gospel of peace

This is the example of how we should walk in this new life that we have been given through the salvation provided to us by Jesus Christ. We are no longer at odds with God. We are no longer sinners but the righteousness of God. Peace is the path that we are now prepared to walk. We live to walk in peace with God, peace with our brothers and sisters in Christ, and peace with all men and women that we shall encounter.

The gospel of Jesus Christ has been called and is considered the good news. As we walk in peace, we live to share this good news with all others. We fight against anything and everything that will come against this path of peace and of the good news of Christ.

The good news about Jesus Christ provides a strong foundation needed to stand firm against the powers of darkness.

Rose Publishing: The Armor of God.

The Shield of Faith

above all, taking the shield of faith, wherewith ye shall be able to quench all the fiery darts of the wicked.

The shield of faith is the weapon that we use to ward off all the attacks of the enemy. These attacks or fiery darts can come in many different forms. They can be negative circumstances, hurtful or harmful words, financial difficulties, relationship breakups or divorce, and sickness or death of a loved one just to name a few. The shield of faith will protect us from all these different types of situations.

The power behind the shield of faith is based on what we attach to our faith. Our faith is attached to God. We have faith in God and his word. We have faith that God's word is true. We have faith that God will fulfill all of his promises. Maintaining these attachments to our faith is what makes the shield of faith impenetrable.

Claiming God's promises by faith, trusting in his unchanging character, and holding up his truth will deflect and extinguish all the enemy's lies. Regardless of the form which these incoming flames take, faith overcomes.

Chip Ingram: The Invisible War

The Helmet of Salvation

And take the helmet of salvation

The helmet of salvation gives us the assurance that we have been delivered from sin. It protects our mind from the condemnation of the enemy. When we put on the helmet of salvation, we know that our lives are connected with the Lord because of his sacrifice at Calvary.

We also know that we are forgiven for our sins and that God is there for us in times of error. The helmet of salvation connects us to God in times of battle and demonic attacks.

O God the Lord, the strength of my salvation, thou hast covered my head in the day of battle.

Psalm 140:7

The Sword of the Spirit

and the sword of the spirit, which is the word of God.

The sword of the spirit is the only offensive weapon described in the biblical passage of Ephesians 6:10 – 17. This passage goes on to describe the sword of the Spirit as being the word of God. The word of God is where we attacked the enemy.

The word of God is what we use against all of Satan's Battle tactics. The word of God also strengthens our shield of faith. Therefore, we must consistently polish and sharpen our sword by studying and ingesting into our spirit the word of God.

So then faith cometh by hearing, and hearing by the word of God

Romans 10:17

For the word of God is quick, and powerful, and sharper than any two-edged sword, piercing even to the dividing asunder of soul and spirit, and of the joints and marrow, and is a discerner of the thoughts and intents of the heart.

Hebrews 4:12

OUR BATTLE TACTICS

In the last chapter we spoke of the power behind the weapons of our warfare, the type of weapons available to us and the purpose behind the weapons that we utilize as we engaged the enemy.

The question that we did not answer is "What are the actual weapons of our warfare?" We did speak about the primary weapon of our warfare which is the sword of the spirit also known as the word of God. This is the chapter where we will discuss our weapons and how we utilize those weapons.

Tactic 1 – Confessions

Earlier, we stated that our confessions were a tactic that the enemy utilized against us. We discussed how we hear negative statements within our society and we unconsciously repeat those statements. We also spoke about the power behind those negative confessions and how Satan use that against us.

Death and life are in the power of the tongue: and they that love it shall eat the fruit thereof.

Proverbs 18:21

Now, we are going to share how we can use the power of our confessions to work on our behalf opposed to the enemy's. Just as the enemy uses negative confessions against us, we can use positive confessions against his tactics. When these positive confessions are combined with the sword of the spirit which is the word of God, they carry a power that all demonic forces must obey.

Just as the enemy can gain ground in the battlefield of your mind when you speak negative confessions, you can take that ground back through the positive confessions that you speak. Our confessions are both a battle tactic and one of the weapons of our warfare.

In the face of all trials, test, temptations, and tribulations, I cut to pieces the snares of the enemy by speaking the word of God.

Germaine Copeland: Prayers That Avail Much

Tactic 2 – Resistance

Resistance is an act of our volition. We must choose to resist the thoughts and attacks of the enemy. We have to do this based on our free will. When we make the choice to resist the enemy's advances, we are exercising a power that will cause the enemy to flee.

Submit yourselves therefore to God. Resist the devil, and he will flee from you.

James 4:7

The key behind the power of resistance is that we submit to God. We have to understand that we must choose to resist, and in that choice, we exercise our spiritual strength. Yet, we do not rely on our strength alone. If we attempt to resist in our own strength, we will fail. Our choice has to be based on God and his word. In that submission unto God we ask and rely on him to empower us as we resist.

Tactic 3 – Prayer

Prayer is the means of how we communicate with God. Earlier, we stated that when we engage in war we must know and understand our enemy. What's more important than knowing the enemy is knowing God, Our Father, Our Commanding Officer in this war who is Our Greatest Advocate. Prayer gives us a direct line to the father through his Holy Spirit which lives on inside of you.

Prayer is the most powerful weapon that we have in this battle. We must know how to pray, and how to use prayer when we engaged the enemy. God's word is full of instructions regarding prayer. We need to study and become familiar with the word of God in regard to prayer as we fight the enemy.

Tactic 4 – Fasting

Fasting is more than just not eating food. When one decides to fast, instead of eating physical food, he feeds on spiritual food. Fasting provides a spiritual cleansing and prepares you to be more in tune with the Lord. When we are attacked by the enemy, fasting is a good way to prepare for the battle.

Once again, the emphasis of fasting is feeding on spiritual food. When you decide to start a fast, especially in times of demonic attacks, you must decide to read God's word; study God's word; and pray during the duration of the fast.

When you eliminate food from your diet for a number of days, your spirit becomes uncluttered by the things of this world and amazingly sensitive to the things of God.

Jentezen Franklin: Fasting

Tactic 5 – Reading God's Word

My people are destroyed for lack of knowledge: because thou hast rejected knowledge, I will also reject thee, that thou shall be no priest to me: seeing thou hast forgotten the law of thy God, I will also forget thy children.

Hosea 4:6

The reading of God's word is the way that we gain the knowledge that is necessary to confront the enemy in times of attacks. Reading God's word is the means of ingesting his word into our spirit. God will not transfer his word to us without participation on our part. The word of God is the Sword of the Spirit. Reading his word teaches us how to use his sword while in battle with the enemy.

Tactic 6 – Studying God's Word

Studying God's word is the enhancement of reading God's word. Reading the word of God is how we ingest his word into our spirit, studying the word of God is how we transfer that knowledge and understanding to our minds. As we stated previously reading the word of God teaches us how to use his sword while in battle with the enemy. Studying the word of God is how we enhance our skill when using the Sword of the Spirit.

Study to show thyself approved unto God, a workman that needeth not to be ashamed, rightly dividing the word of truth.

2 Timothy 2:15

Tactic 7 – Love

Love has been described as one of the most powerful emotions. God's word also commands us to love one another because God is love. This command is often very difficult to follow because in many cases we do not want to love someone who does not show us that love in return.

Yet what makes love such a powerful battle tactic is that the deceptions of the enemy cannot penetrate a heart that is full of God's love. There are a variety of different descriptions for the types of love a person can possess. The four most well-known are:

1. Agape – The love of God; unconditional love
2. Eros – Sexual or passionate love
3. Philia – Friendship goodwill
4. Storge– Familial love; love between parents and children

When in the mist of spiritual warfare, you must focus on the agape love. Your love must be unconditional and not focused on behaviors or circumstances. The best way to apply this love is first to pray and ask God to fill you with his love and next to focus on the spirit of the person and not their behavior or the circumstances that involves them.

Beloved, let us love one another: for love is of God; and everyone that loveth is born of God, and knoweth God. He that loveth not knoweth not God; for God is love.

1 John 4:7, 8

Tactic 8 – Patience

An ability or willingness to suppress restlessness or annoyance when confronted with delay. Dictionary.com

There is a popular saying to never pray for patience because you just might get it. This saying is based on the belief that in order to develop patience you have to be expose to negative situations and circumstances that won't go away. However, God's word states on numerous occasions for us to have patience.

This saying is a satanic deception design to keep you from developing a most powerful virtue of God. Patience is usually associated with some form of waiting. That waiting could be for an answered prayer, a grocery line, or numerous other things. Being patient is a command of God. The enemy attempts to come against you in times of impatience by convincing you to act outside of God's timing.

Yet with patience you can withstand those demonic thoughts. The virtue of patience combined with the shield of faith and the tactic of resistance will cause the enemy to flee. Do not fear any negative situation or circumstance but use it as a means of developing and strengthening your patience.

And not only so, but we glory in tribulations also: knowing that tribulation worketh patience; and patience, experience; and experience, hope: and hope maketh not ashamed; because of the love of God is shed abroad in our hearts by the Holy Ghost which is given unto us.

Romans 5:3 – 5

Tactic 9 – Praise

Praise is not something that we would normally consider as a battle tactic but through scripture God's word speaks about praising God and the powerful effects of offering your praises to him. Earlier we spoke about one of the ways to prepare when you are facing a demonic attack is by fasting.

Praise falls into that same category. When under attack start praising God. Praise is about thanksgiving. Thanking God for his goodness and blessing. Praising God will calm your spirit and help you to focus. Focusing on God's goodness and not the spiritual attack that you are facing. Once your spirit is calm and in tune with God you are in a better position to utilize your other battle tactics as you confront the enemy.

By him therefore let us offer the sacrifice of praise to God continually, that is, the fruits of our lips giving thanks to his name.

Hebrews 3:15

Now that we have shared with you our Battle tactics, there may be a couple of things that you have noticed. First, we shared with you more tactics that Satan uses against you than the tactics you have to engage and fight against the enemy. Second, we described the different battle tactics that we have but we didn't go into detail about how to use these tactics. Now we are going to address those two issues.

First the reason why we shared more of the enemy's tactics is because the enemy has already lost the war and needs more tactics to deceive you into giving him ground. When we engage in battle, it is not to take ground from the enemy but to reclaim ground that was stolen. The ground gained by the enemy was already ours. We were either deceived or we had a lack of knowledge which is the reason why the enemy was able to gain ground.

The reason we have less battle tactics than the enemy is we already have won the war. We are aligned with the Trinity: God; Jesus Christ; and the Holy Spirit. Due to Jesus' sacrifice, the authority which God originally gave man has been reclaimed. The only way Satan can gain any ground is through deception and lies.

Now that we know what our Battle tactics are, how do we use them? The most powerful way to use our Battle tactics is in combination. When we are under attack by the enemy, demonic forces don't just come against us utilizing one tactic. They come against us utilizing a variety of tactics with the overall goal of overwhelming us to a point of surrender.

The enemy will orchestrate a negative circumstance; plant negative thoughts in our mind; influenced a close loved one to verbally validate those negative thoughts; play on your feelings of doubt and fear; and orchestrate different circumstances designed to enhance those feelings. All these fiery darts will come at you simultaneously with the purpose of breaking you down to a point of surrender.

When we engage the enemy and use our Battle tactics, we must come against the enemy in the same manner. When that first fiery darts has been thrown at you, you have to be clear about your spiritual armor. Once your spiritual armor is on you take the sword of the spirit and come against the attack by confessing the word of God. You may need to fast in order to clear your spirit and be in a better position to hear from God.

Pray and get God's guidance during this demonic attack. Resist any thoughts or circumstances that are contrary to God's word. Confess again the word of God as you come against that demonic attack. We have to use our Battle tactics in combination as we come against the enemy. These are just examples of how we must use our Battle tactics and spiritual weapons. We cannot take these attacks lightly. This is serious and we have to stand firm and not allow the enemy to take any ground.

COMBAT TECHNIQUES

STANDING ON OUR VICTORY

Victory – A success or triumph over an enemy in battle or war.

Dictionary.com

Throughout this writing we have consistently stated that we have the victory over the enemy in this battle. Yet, we are constantly speaking about battle tactics of the enemy, our spiritual armor, and tactics that we can used against him in this war. Although we have explained in the earlier chapter why we need to be knowledgeable in these areas; it's important that we emphasize why we have victory.

We need to know and understand that we are fighting from a victorious position and not from a position of uncertainty. We are fighting from a position of strength and not weakness. All this leads to the question: Why do we have the victory? The simple answer to this question is we have the victory because God said we have the victory in his word. God's intentions regarding the results of this war was prophesize in Isaiah 25:7,8

And he will destroy in this mountain the face of the covering cast over all people, and the vail that is spread over all nations. He will swallow up death in victory; and the Lord God will wipe away tears from off all faces; and the rebuke of his people shall he take away from off all the earth: for the Lord hath spoken it.

Isaiah 25:7,8

God's word also shares that we have overcome the world due to our belief in Jesus Christ's sacrifice and death upon the cross at Calvary.

For whatsoever is born of God overcometh the world: and this is the victory that overcometh the world, even our faith. Who is he that overcometh the world, but he that believeth that Jesus is the Son of God?

1 John 5:4,5

Additionally, God's word reemphasizes the prophesy stated in Isaiah 25:7,8 when it speaks of Christ's return and how death will no longer reign over the believers in 1 Corinthians 15: 51-54 of the new testament. What is also stated in 1 Corinthians 15 is that God has given us the victory through our Lord Jesus Christ.

But thanks be to God, which giveth us the victory through our Lord Jesus Christ.

1 Corinthians 15:57

Another reason we can be confident in our victory is that we are aligned with God's powerful army who is fighting on our behalf. When I look at the army of God, I focus on three elements of the army. First and foremost is the trinity, the Father; the Son; and the Holy Spirit.

The Father who created all that exist in the universe. The son who sacrifice his life in order to reclaim what man had lost. He defeated the enemy and provided salvation to mankind. The Holy Spirit who was given to teach and give us guidance regarding God's word and his will for our lives.

Next is God's heavenly angels who fought beside God as he casted Satan and his demonic forces out of heaven. Angels are the servants of God created to enforce his will. God's Angels will protect us and fight on our behalf

The angel of the Lord encampeth round about them that fear him, and delivereth them.

Psalm 34:7

There shall no evil befall thee, neither shall any plague come nigh thy dwelling. For he shall give his angels charge over thee, to keep thee in all thy ways. They shall bear thee up in their hands, lest thou dash thy foot against a stone.

Psalm 91 10-12

The final element of God's army is a resource that many choose not to take advantage of is the fellow believers. The reason behind people choosing not to take advantage of this resource when engaged in spiritual warfare is that in many cases, they may be able to look back to an area of their past where they were let down or failed by a fellow believer.

This is the point where I tell you to get over it! In this war that we have with the enemy, you can't afford to disregard this powerful resource. In the community of believers, you will develop several different types of relationships. You develop casual relationships based on your common beliefs.

Personal relationships which are based on friendships and a genuine concern for the people. Finally, there are those relationships that goes beyond just a personal friendship. These are the bonds that form the type of brotherhood and sisterhood that will support you while in the frontlines of the battlefield.

This final category of relationship of believers are the ones that you take with you into battle. Generally, you will find that there will be less people that you may know in this category than any of the others. When you find people, who falls into this category of believers you must cherish and continue to develop those relationships. These are lifelong bonds. This is a powerful element of your army as you battle and oppose Satan's demonic forces.

Therefore, we have to be confident in the assurance that we are fighting from a position of victory and not weakness when we are confronted with the demonic attacks of the enemy. We cannot allow ourselves to become discouraged when the fiery darts of the enemy is hurled towards us. We can never give in to fear, doubt, or any of the other numerous tactics that the enemy will attempt to use.

EXERCISING OUR AUTHORITY

This is where the rubber meets the road. When it comes to exercising our Authority, there are a few things that you need to know. First, the authority that we have comes from God. In the Garden of Eden, God gave Adam the authority to rule over and take dominion of the earth.

And God bless them, and God said unto them, be fruitful, and multiply, and replenish the earth, and subdue it: and have dominion over the fish of the sea, and over the fowl of the air, and over every living thing that moveth upon the earth.

Genesis 1:28

And God said, let us make man in our image, after our likeness: and let them have dominion over the fish of the sea, over the fowl of the air, and over the cattle, and over all the earth, and over every creeping thing that creepeth upon the earth.

Genesis 1:26

God's authority over the earth was a God-given right for mankind. However, that right was lost because of Adam's disobedience in the garden of Eden. Mankind lost the authority to have dominion over the earth and Satan claimed it.

And the devil said unto him, all this power will I give thee, and the glory of them: for that is delivered unto me; and to whomsoever I will I give it.

Luke 4:6

Yet there was a plan and that plan was the gift of salvation through Jesus Christ. The sacrifice of Jesus on the cross at Calvary paved the way for the redemption of mankind. Jesus reclaimed the authority which was lost by Adam and has made it available to all who believe in his name and accept him as the only begotten Son of God.

For if by one man's offense death reigned by one; much more they which receive abundance of grace and of the gift of righteousness shall reign in life by one, Jesus Christ. Therefore, by the offence of one judgment came upon all men to condemnation; even so by the righteous of one the gift came upon all men unto justification of life. For as by one man's disobedience many were made sinners, so by the obedience of one shall many be made righteous.

Romans 5:17-19

And Jesus came and spake unto them, saying, All power is given unto me in heaven and in earth.

Matthew 28:18

Now that we know the history of our God given authority, let's explore the power of our authority and how we can use it during spiritual attacks from the enemy. We can start by answering the question:

What is Authority?

Authority – a power or right delegated or given

In the book "The Believer's Authority" by Kenneth E. Hagin, he simplified the definition by saying that authority was "Delegated Power". That power has been delegated to us as believers in Jesus' crucifixion and resurrection. What must be remembered is that this is not your power, this is the power of God.

A man with authority to use the name of Jesus is one of the most powerful individuals on the earth today – far more powerful than evil spirits, demons, principalities, powers, or rulers of darkness.

Charles Capps: Authority in Three Worlds.

This is the power that has already defeated Satan and his demons. You have just been given the right to use it. We not only have the right to use this power but scripture commands us to do so.

Behold, I give unto you power to tread on serpents and scorpions, and over all the power of the enemy: and nothing shall by any means hurt you.

Luke 10:19

Finally, my brethren, be strong in the Lord, and in the power of his might. Put on the whole armor of God, that ye may be able to sand against the wiles of the devil. For we wrestle not against flesh and blood, but against principalities, against powers, against the rulers of darkness of this world, against spiritual wickedness in high places.

Ephesians 6:10-12

Our authority is what enables us to fight from a position of strength and victory. Now that we understand the history and the power behind our authority, we will venture into how to exercise our authority in times of spiritual warfare. As we stated earlier our authority comes from God.

When we exercise our authority, we are standing behind the power of God. We must have faith and confidence in that power when we confront the enemy. Additionally, we must understand the limits of our authority.

We can exercise authority over the enemy and demonic spirits, but we can't exercise authority over the free will of man. So how do we exercise our authority? The simple answer is by speaking the word of God.

We confess God's word regarding situations and circumstances that is contrary to his will for your life. We confess God's word to demonic spirits that attack you. We speak God's word with boldness and confidence while reminding and commanding the enemy that he must obey. We stand in our authority anytime we use any of our battle tactics when confronting the enemy.

When we exercise our authority, we are standing behind the power of God. We must have faith and confidence in that power when we confront the enemy. Additionally, we must understand the limits of our authority.

And now, Lord, behold their threatening: and grant unto thy servants, that with all boldness they may speak thy word,

Acts 4:29

FIGHTING ON BEHALF OF OTHERS

Now that we have learned how to fight the enemy in spiritual warfare, the next step is to learn how to fight on behalf of others. The first step in fighting for others is sharing knowledge. The information that has been shared in this book is considered the meat of the word. This is not spiritual milk for feeding the babes in Christ, this is for the spiritually mature. Now that you have digested this information, you have an obligation to share it with others.

Sharing Knowledge

Sharing the knowledge of the information contained in this writing is not just giving them a book and telling them to read it. If you truly want to fight on the behalf of another you will have to engage with them. As a Curriculum Developer and Instructional Systems Specialist, there were two things that I always focused on when educating another.

First you need to focus on the transfer of knowledge and then you have to be familiar with the foundational principles of the subject matter.

When dealing with the transfer of knowledge you really need to take a look at where the person is mentally in regard to the subject matter. You have to reach down to where there are at and bring them up to your level of knowledge.

Regarding foundational principles you have to be certain that the person you are teaching understand these principles before moving to the more advance material. As stated earlier, the information in this writing is considered the meat of the word. Prior to getting into this material, you have to be certain that they have been fed the spiritual milk and understand those foundational principles.

Intercession

Next when fighting on behalf of others you must be prepared to intercede on their behalf. Until such time as they learn how to fight these spiritual battles for themselves, you must be willing to use your authority and implore all the battle tactics that you have learned for them.

The Prayer of Agreement

Joining with them in the prayer of agreement is a powerful way to fight alongside individuals who are unable to fight for themselves.

Again I say unto you, That if two of you shall agree on earth as touching anything that they shall ask, it shall be done for them of my Father which is in heaven. For where two or three are gathered together in my name, there am I in the midst of them.

Matthew 18:19,20

Battle Alliances

Previously, we stated that as believers we develop different type of relationships. One of the types that we spoke about were those brotherhood and sisterhood relationships that are lifelong bonds. These are the people that you take with you into the battlefield. Although you may not have many of these types of relationships it is hopeful that everyone has at least two people who can fall in this category. This is your battle alliance.

When fighting on the behalf of others you should include them into your battle alliance until they have the opportunity to develop their own. While they are aligned with you and those in your battle alliance you should continue to educate them and cultivate the relationship that you have with them. Additionally, you have to teach them to cultivate their own relationships so that they can have their own battle alliances.

THINGS TO REMEMBER

Now that we have completed this book on Spiritual Martial Arts, you are officially prepared for battle. There are certain things that you must consistently review as a frontline member of God's spiritual army.

1. Know your enemy.

Thus, we may say that if you know yourself and know your enemy, you will gain victory a hundred times out of a hundred. If you know yourself but do not know your enemy, you will meet one defeat for every victory. If you know neither yourself nor your enemy, you will never be victorious.

Sun Tzu: The Art of War

The enemy that you face goes by many names but primarily by Satan and the devil. He is a master of deception and his sole purpose is your destruction.

Be sober, be vigilant; Because your adversary the devil, as a roaring lion, walketh about, seeking whom he may devour.

1 Peter 5: 8

2. The Enemy's Battle Tactics

There are numerous tactics that Satan utilizes against the believer. His goal is to kill steal and destroy our lives.

a. Deception
b. Doubt
c. Circumstances of Life
d. Passivity
e. Sin
f. Intellect & Reasoning
g. Desires
h. Fear
i. Money
j. Pride
k. Relationships

    l. Confessions
   m. Feelings
   n. Unanswered Prayer
   o. Dreams

3. Spiritual Espionage

The term spiritual espionage refers to the aspect of our lives that provides information to the enemy concerning who we are and our individual desires.

This aspect can be considered to be in partnership with the agenda of the enemy. These are subtle attacks that we don't even realize with a purpose to cause us to rebel against the will of God. Areas of spiritual espionage includes:

1. Desires
2. Passivity
3. Pride
4. Relationships
5. Intellect/Reasoning

4. Weapons of our Warfare

We must understand the power behind our weapons. We need to understand the type of weapons available to us. Finally, we must know the purpose of our weapons in order to effectively use them against the enemy.

For the weapons of our warfare are not carnal, but mighty through God to the pulling down of strongholds; Casting down imaginations, and every high thing that exalteth itself against the knowledge of God, and bringing into captivity every thought to the obedience of Christ;

2 Corinthians 10:4,5

5. Our Battle Tactics

Just as the enemy has battle tactics that he utilizes against us, we have battle tactics that we can use to fight against his attacks.

a. Confession
b. Resistance
c. Prayer
d. Fasting
e. Reading God's word
f. Studying God's word
g. Love
h. Patience
i. Praise

6. Standing on Our Victory

We need to know and understand that we are fighting from a victorious position and not from a position of uncertainty. We are fighting from a position of strength and not weakness. God's word shares that we have overcome the world due to our belief in Jesus Christ's sacrifice and death upon the cross at Calvary.

Another reason we can be confident in our victory is that we are aligned with God's powerful army who is fighting on our behalf. When I look at the army of God, I focus on three elements of the army. First and foremost is the trinity, the Father; the Son; and the Holy Spirit.

Next is God's heavenly angels who fought beside God as he casted Satan and his demonic forces out of heaven. Angels are the servants of God created to enforce his will. God's Angels will protect us and fight on our behalf.

The final element of God's army is a resource that many choose not to take advantage of is the fellow believers. In this war that we have with the enemy, you can't afford to disregard this powerful resource. This is a powerful element of your army as you battle an oppose Satan's demonic forces.

7. Exercising Our Authority

When it comes to exercising our Authority, there are a few things that you need to know. First, the authority that we have comes from God. What must be remembered is that this is not your power, this is the power of God.

A man with authority to use the name of Jesus is one of the most powerful individuals on the earth today – far more powerful than evil spirits, demons, principalities, powers, or rulers of darkness.

Charles Capps: Authority in Three Worlds.

This is the power that has already defeated Satan and his demons. You have just been given the right to use it. When we exercise our authority, we are standing behind the power of God. We must have faith and confidence in that power when we confront the enemy.

8. Fighting on Behalf of Others

Now that we have learned how to fight the enemy in spiritual warfare, the next step is to learn how to fight on behalf of others. There are several things that you can do as you fight on the behalf of others.

Sharing Knowledge

Sharing the knowledge of the information contained in this writing is not just giving them a book and telling them to read it. If you truly want to fight on the behalf of another you will have to engage with them.

Intercession

Next when fighting on behalf of others you must be prepared to intercede on their behalf. Until such time as they learn how to fight these spiritual battles for themselves, you must be willing to use your authority and implore all the battle tactics that you have learned for them.

The Prayer of Agreement

Joining with them in the prayer of agreement is a powerful way to fight alongside individuals who are unable to fight for themselves.

Battle Alliances

When fighting on the behalf of others you should include them into your battle alliance until they have the opportunity to develop their own. While they are aligned with you and those in your battle alliance you should continue to educate them and cultivate the relationship that you have with them. Additionally, you have to teach them to cultivate their own relationships so that they can have their own battle alliance.

Guidance

Finally, something that must be shared in this writing is what was shared in my previous book *Grace Mercy & Faith: The Keys to Spiritual Empowerment.*

Whenever you read a book such as this which is based on God's word as contained in the Bible, the information contained in the book can be misinterpreted as directly coming from the word of God as opposed to guidance based on the study of God's word. This book is not doctrine, the doctrine is the Bible, "God's word".

This book is guidance. Guidance based on the doctrine. There are no rules or regulations regarding following the information in this book or any other book you may read that is based on the word of God, but wisdom dictates that you follow the guidance so that you can live a better life.

BEFORE YOU GO ANY FURTHER

While this information is fresh in your mind please take the time to share with us your thoughts by giving us a review at the following website: https://www.amazon.com/dp/B07WZB9B49

Ministers and Ministries.

If you would like to share the message contained within the pages of this book, you can order it at deeply discounted rates for members of the Clergy at our website:

https://wwww.curriculumsystem.com/the-battle-is-on.html

ENLIST IN THE
SPIRITUAL ARMY OF GOD!

Now that you have completed "The Battle is on!" make a commitment to fight on the behalf of those who are unable to fight for themselves.

Sign up as a Spiritual Martial Artist and receive the following:

1. Spiritual Martial Arts Certificate of Completion
   https://wwww.curriculumsystem.com/spiritual-martial-arts-2.html
2. Access to Fighting on Behalf of Others Curriculum
   https://wwww.curriculumsystem.com/fighting-on-behalf-of-others.html
3. Discount on the Grace Mercy & Faith book Series
   https://wwww.curriculumsystem.com/spiritual-martial-arts.html
4. Distribution rights on selected Products from the Curriculum & Training Systems website.
   https://wwww.curriculumsystem.com/grace-mercy-faith-3.html

FROM THE PEN OF LANCE DICKSON

https://wwww.curriculumsystem.com/grace-mercy-faith.html

https://wwww.curriculumsystem.com/10-commandment-of-belief.html

https://wwww.curriculumsystem.com/study-to-show-thyself-approved.html

Grace
Mercy &
Faith

The Study Guide

Lance Dickson

https://wwww.curriculumsystem.com/the-study-guide.html

Made in the USA
Columbia, SC
25 November 2019

83809681R00048